Highlights™

W9-AXN-464

BRIDGING GRADES

P&K

Summer
Big Fun Workbook

For information about permission to reproduce selections from this book for
an entire school or school district, please contact permissions@highlights.com.

Published by Highlights Learning • 815 Church Street • Honesdale, Pennsylvania 18431
ISBN: 978-1-68437-288-1
Mfg. 01/2019
Printed in Guangzhou, Guangdong, China
First edition
10 9 8 7 6 5 4 3 2 1

For assistance in the preparation of this book, the editors would like to thank:
Vanessa Maldonado, MSEd; MS Literacy Ed. K–12; Reading/LA Consultant Cert.; K–5 Literacy Instructional Coach
Kristin Ward, MS Curriculum, Instruction, and Assessment; K–5 Mathematics Instructional Coach
Jump Start Press, Inc.

Say No to Summer Slide . . .

Your child's summer learning adventure starts here!

This book is divided into eight chapters, each designed to bridge preschool and kindergarten and give your child practice in a variety of curriculum areas all summer long.

Tips for using this book with your child:

1 **Find the right time.**
Whenever possible, start new activities in the morning, following a snack or meal, or after a nap—any time she is well fed and rested.

2 **Let your child take the lead.**
If your child is eager to keep going, encourage him to do so, but don't pressure him to complete a certain number of pages or even finish an activity.

3 **Take it with you.**
Learning can happen anywhere. Bring this book with you during your summertime travels for learn-on-the-go fun in the car, on a plane, or even in the backyard.

4 **Pour on the praise.**
When your child works hard on an activity, acknowledge her efforts enthusiastically. She'll love that you're excited, and she'll be happy about her efforts and actions.

5 **Join the fun.**
At the end of each chapter is a bonus activity, such as a recipe, craft, or science project. You can also extend the learning by playing math games—using dominoes, dice, or a deck of cards—and by encouraging your child to notice letters and words on signs at stores or when you go for a walk.

and Yes to Big Fun!

As your child journeys through the book, she can track her progress by placing stickers on the **Summer Big Fun Adventure Poster**.

Here's how:

1 Remove the poster from the back of the book and unfold it. Hang it up or place it on a flat surface.

2 To advance along the path, your child will complete the activities in a chapter of the book.

3 When your child has completed a chapter, he will place that chapter's sticker from the sticker sheet on the correct signpost on the poster.

4 Once your child has placed all eight signpost stickers, she has completed her journey and earned her Achievement Certificate.

BONUS FUN!

The colorful spray-park poster is also a Hidden Pictures® puzzle! It is hiding 20 bubble wands for your child to find.

 Each time your child finishes a chapter, add a sticker!

 Place a sun sticker on each hidden bubble wand!

 Use the emoji stickers to mark favorite activities in the book!

3

Contents

Each chapter covers a variety of subjects, so that kids will get practice in different curriculum areas throughout the summer and be ready for kindergarten.

Don't forget!

Your Hidden Pictures® poster and stickers are at the back of this book!

4

Go Fetch!

Trace the line from each dog to its treat. Which dog is the biggest?

Aa

This is an uppercase A.

This is a lowercase a.

Trace the uppercase **A**. Then write your own.

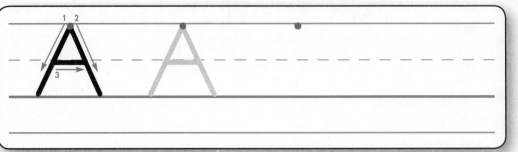

Trace the lowercase **a**. Then write your own.

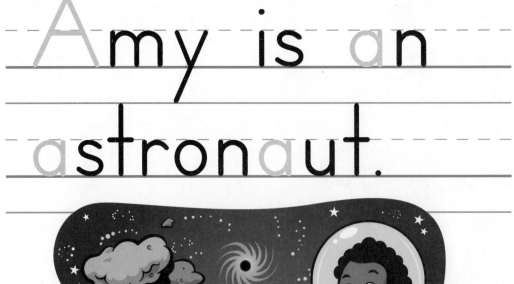

Now trace **A** and **a** to finish the sentence.

Amy is an astronaut.

I

one

This is the number I.

This is the word **one**.

This is one way to show I.

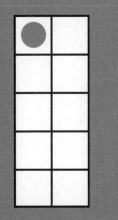

Trace the number I. Then write your own.

Trace the word **one**. Then write your own.

one

Circle the spaceships with just I alien in them. Then draw a line between the 2 that match.

Dino Colors

Color each dinosaur with one of the colors shown on the crayons. Then draw a line from each crayon to the dinosaur whose color matches.

Find the 5 objects in this Hidden Pictures® puzzle.

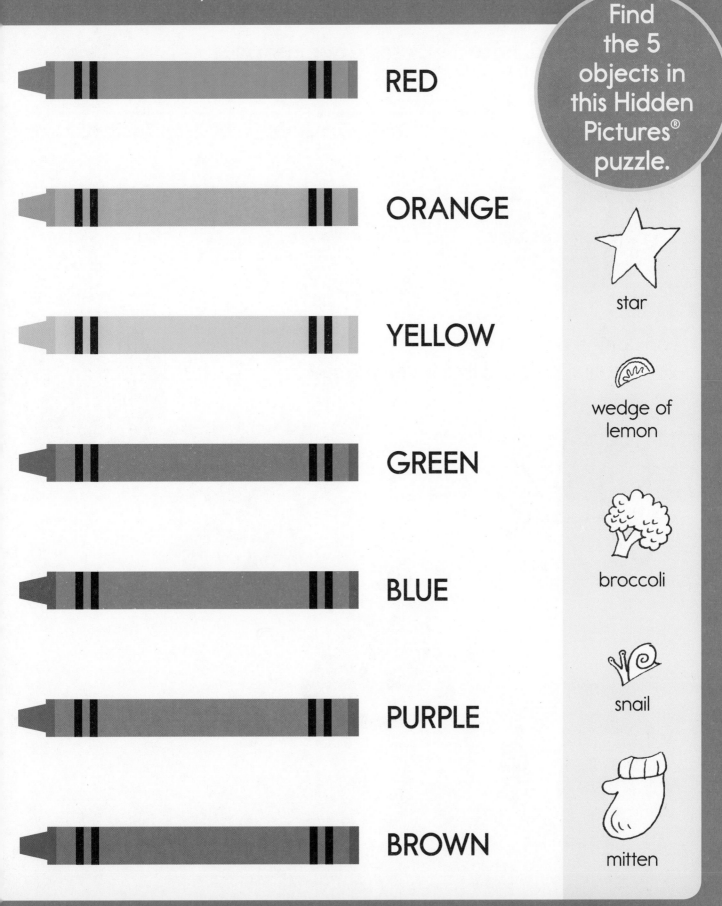

RED

ORANGE

YELLOW

GREEN

BLUE

PURPLE

BROWN

star

wedge of lemon

broccoli

snail

mitten

Circles

A circle is round. Trace the circles. Color them **blue**.

Look at the pictures below.
Draw a circle around the circles you see.

Name something else that is a circle.

2
two

This is the number 2.

This is the word two.

This is one way to show 2.

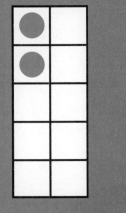

What shape are the spots on the dogs?

Trace the number **2**. Then write your own.

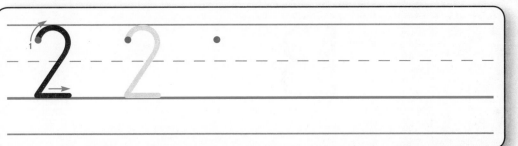

Trace the word **two**. Then write your own.

two

Circle the dog with only **2** spots. Then draw a line between the **2** dogs that match.

Bb

This is an uppercase B.

This is a lowercase b.

Trace the uppercase **B**. Then write your own.

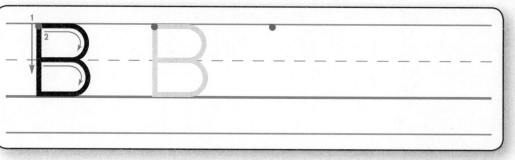

Trace the lowercase **b**. Then write your own.

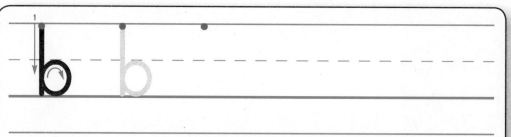

Now trace **B** and **b** to finish the sentence.

Bob kicks
the ball.

Squares

A square has 4 sides that are the same. Trace the squares. Color them green.

Look at the pictures below.
Draw a square around the squares you see.

Name something else that is a square.

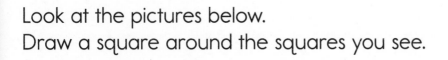

3
three

This is the number 3.

This is the word three.

This is one way to show 3.

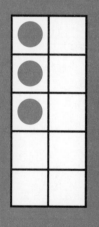

Trace the number **3**. Then write your own.

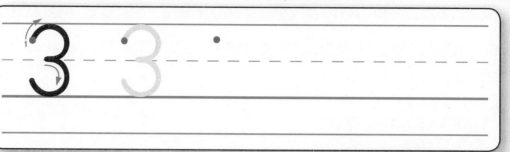

Trace the word **three**. Then write your own.

Count the **3** cows. Then follow the path with **3**'s to lead them to the barn.

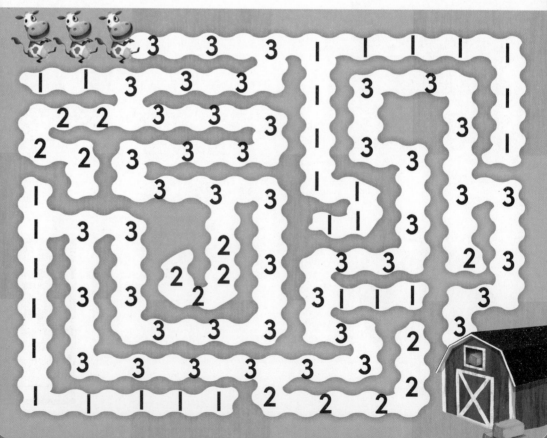

Cc

This is an uppercase C.

This is a lowercase c.

Trace the uppercase **C**. Then write your own.

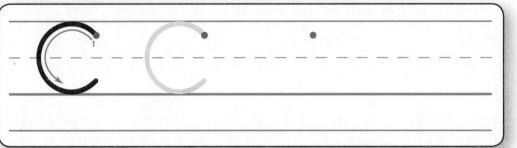

Trace the lowercase **c**. Then write your own.

Now trace **C** and **c** to finish the sentence.

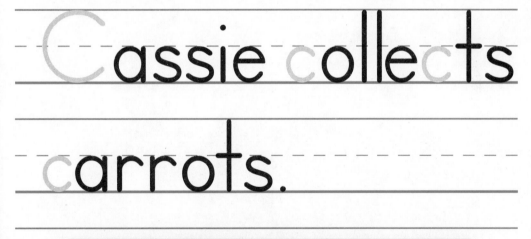

Cassie collects

carrots.

Counting: 1 to 3

Find and count: **1** seashell, **2** kites, **3** bows.
Then find the **3** objects in this Hidden Pictures® puzzle.

toothbrush   crescent moon   bowling ball

Kite Patterns

Which kite comes next? Circle the kite that completes the pattern in each row.

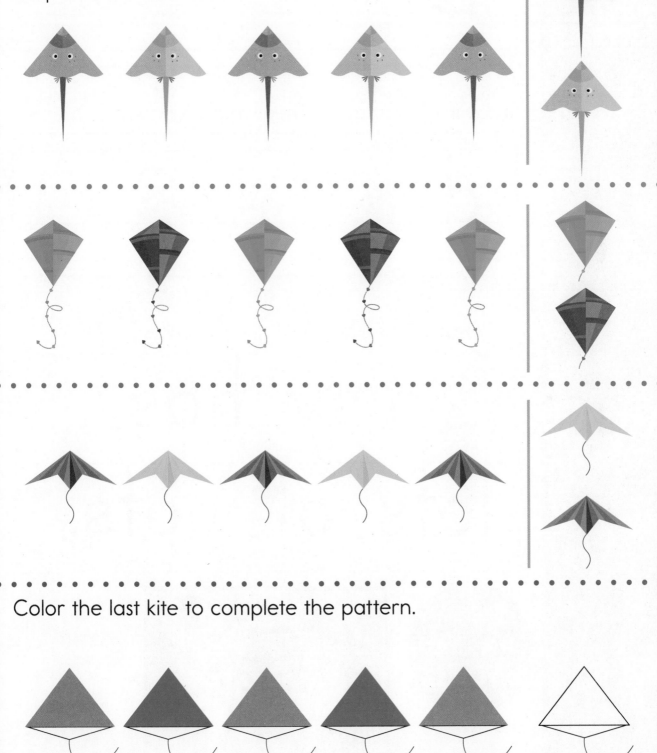

Color the last kite to complete the pattern.

Dd

This is an uppercase D.

This is a lowercase d.

Trace the uppercase **D**. Then write your own.

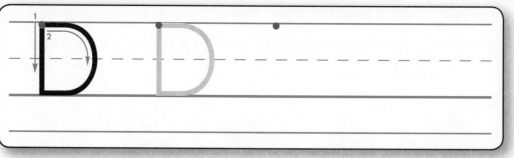

Trace the lowercase **d**. Then write your own.

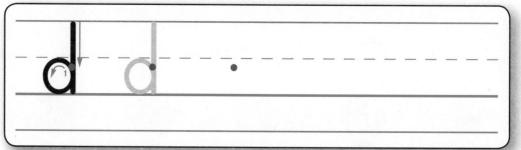

Now trace **D** and **d** to finish the sentence.

Daisy has lots of dots.

Count the dots on Daisy.

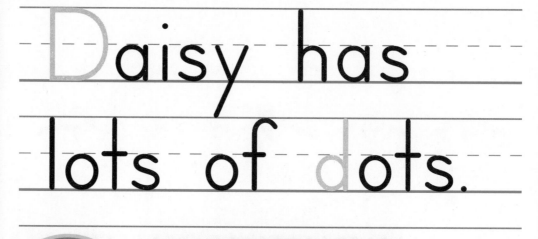

Shape Patterns

Which shape comes next? Circle the shape that completes the pattern in each row.

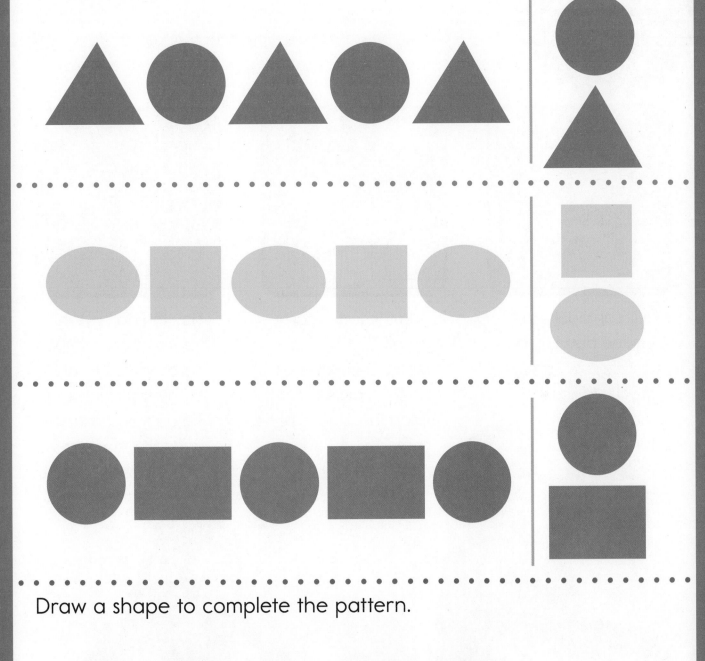

Draw a shape to complete the pattern.

Congratulations! You've completed **Chapter 1**. Place your Chapter 1 sticker on your poster. Try this activity, then start **Chapter 2**!

Traveling Tic-Tac-Toe

YOU WILL NEED:

- Bandanna (or a square piece of fabric)
- Masking tape   • 5 index cards   • Scissors   • Markers

1. With an adult's help, lay the bandanna or fabric square on a flat surface. Use masking tape to form a large tic-tac-toe grid.

2. Fold the index cards in half. Cut on the folded line. Put an *X* on five cards. Put an *O* on the other five cards.

3. Play the game. When you're done, put the cards in the middle of the bandanna. Tie up the corners and take the game with you when you're on the go!

What does it mean to be a good sport?

Trace the lines from each meerkat to its room.

Ee

This is an uppercase E.

This is a lowercase e.

Trace the uppercase **E**. Then write your own.

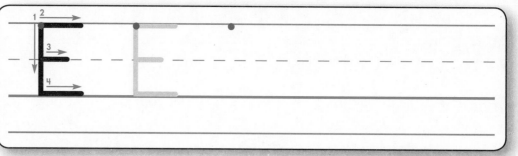

Trace the lowercase **e**. Then write your own.

Now trace **E** and **e** to finish the sentence.

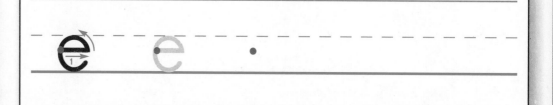

Eva gathers

eggs.

Count and circle 4 eggs.

4
four

This is the number 4.

This is the word **four**.

This is one way to show 4.

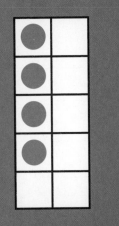

Can you name 4 other kinds of fruit?

Trace the number 4. Then write your own.

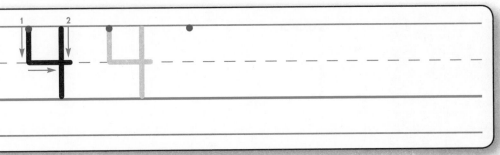

Trace the word **four**. Then write your own.

four

Count and circle 4 oranges. Count and circle 4 bananas.

Ff

This is an uppercase F.

This is a lowercase f.

Trace the uppercase **F**. Then write your own.

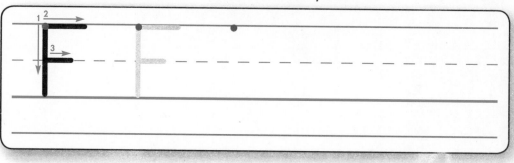

Trace the lowercase **f**. Then write your own.

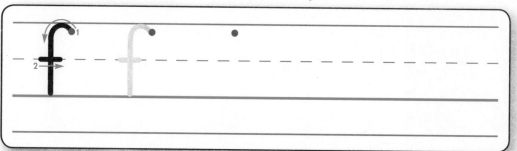

Now trace **F** and **f** to finish the sentence.

Felix fixes food.

Red Apples

Color the apples red. Then find and circle the **6** objects in this Hidden Pictures® puzzle.

lime   paper clip   star   fork   football   belt

5
five

This is the number **5**.

This is the word **five**.

This is one way to show **5**.

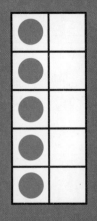

Trace the number **5**. Then write your own.

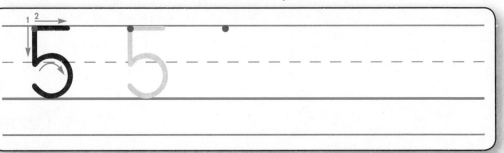

Trace the word **five**. Then write your own.

five

Count the **5** lizards. Then follow the path of **5**'s to help Larry find his friends.

Gg

This is an uppercase G.

This is a lowercase g.

Trace the uppercase **G**. Then write your own.

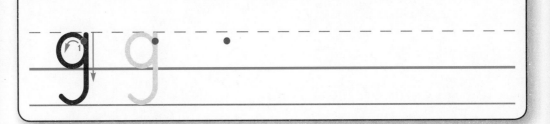

Trace the lowercase **g**. Then write your own.

Now trace **G** and **g** to finish the sentence.

Gilda is a gecko.

Yellow Ducks

Color the ducks yellow. Then find and circle the 6 objects in this Hidden Pictures® puzzle.

lamp

slice of pie

sock

stamp

bread

clock

six

This is the number 6.

This is the word **six**.

This is one way to show 6.

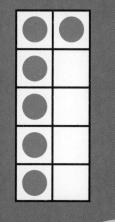

What is another animal that starts with H?

Trace the number **6**. Then write your own.

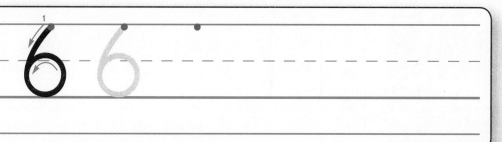

Trace the word **six**. Then write your own.

six

Count the **6** crayons. Then use your own crayons to color this horse.

Hh

This is an uppercase **H**.

This is a lowercase **h**.

Trace the uppercase **H**. Then write your own.

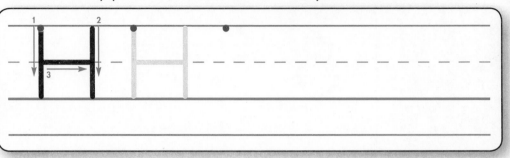

Trace the lowercase **h**. Then write your own.

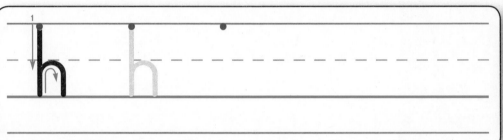

Now trace **H** and **h** to finish the sentence.

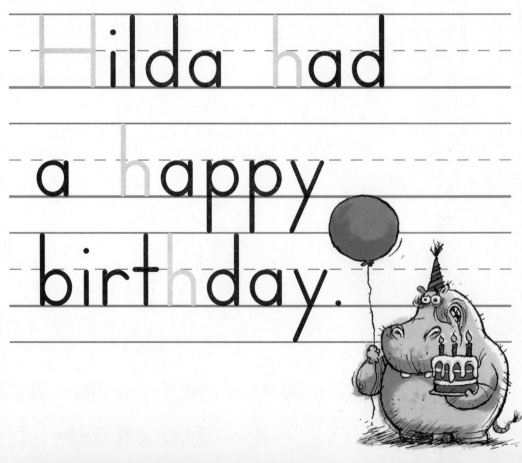

Hilda had a happy birthday.

Build a triangle out of 3 pencils.

A triangle has 3 sides. Trace the triangles. Color them **red**.

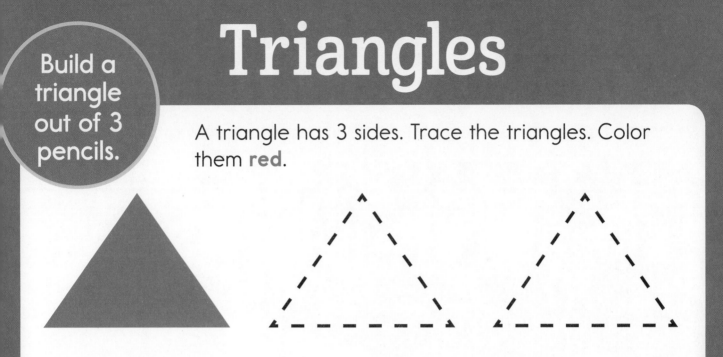

Look at the pictures below.
Draw a triangle around each triangle you see.

Counting: 4 to 6

Find and count: **4** penguins, **5** people, **6** pigeons. Cross off as you count.

Pattern Maze

Follow this pattern to help Zeep get to his spaceship.

I i

This is an uppercase **I**.

This is a lowercase **i**.

Trace the uppercase **I**. Then write your own.

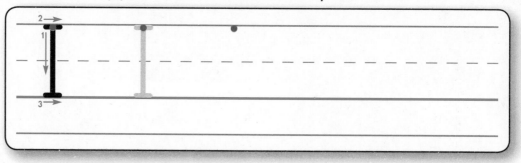

Trace the lowercase **i**. Then write your own.

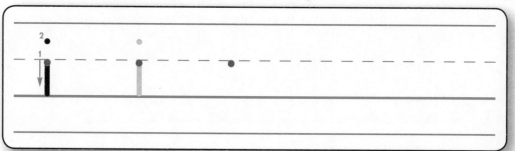

Now trace **I** and **i** to finish the sentence.

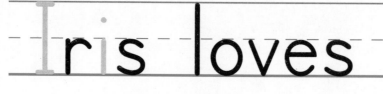

Iris loves

ice cream.

Iris also loves patterns. What scoop should she add on top?

Rectangles

A rectangle has 2 long sides that are the same and 2 short sides that are the same. Trace the rectangles. Color them yellow.

Look at the pictures below.
Draw a rectangle around each rectangle you see.

Complete the Pattern

What shape comes next? Draw a shape and color it in to complete each pattern.

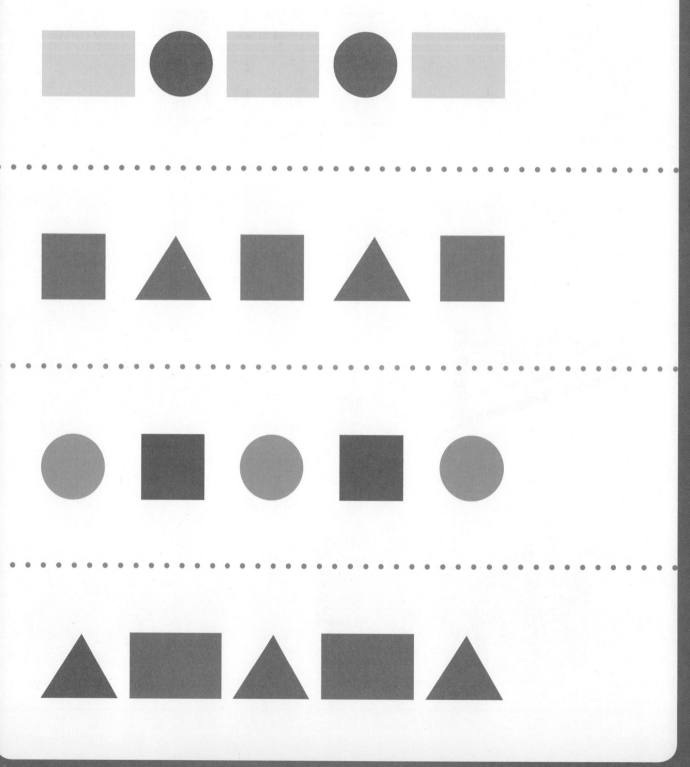

BONUS!
Summer Science Activity

Will a Clay Boat Float?

YOU WILL NEED:

• Modeling clay • Bowl • Water • Pennies

1. With an adult's permission, roll a piece of modeling clay into a ball. Gently drop it into a bowl of water. What happens?

2. Use another piece of clay to make a boat with a large bottom and short sides.

3. Gently set the clay boat onto the water. What happens?

Why do you think boats float?

4. Experiment to see how much weight the boat can carry. Add pennies to the boat until it sinks.

Jj

This is an uppercase **J**.

This is a lowercase **j**.

Trace the uppercase **J**. Then write your own.

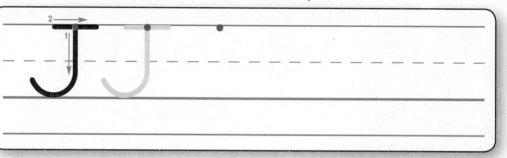

Trace the lowercase **j**. Then write your own.

Now trace **J** and **j** to finish the sentence.

Jack juggles fruit.

How many pieces of fruit is Jack juggling?

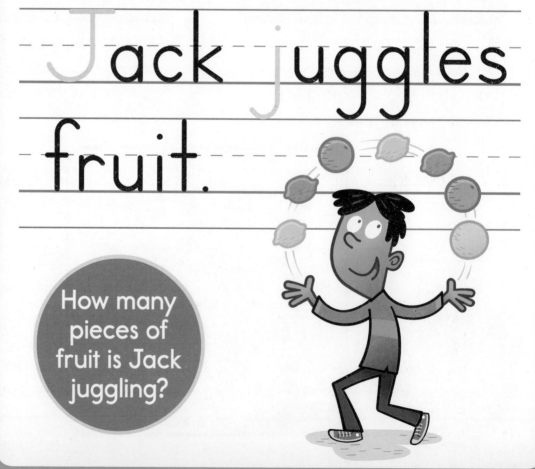

7
seven

This is the number 7.

This is the word **seven**.

This is one way to show 7.

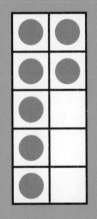

Trace the number **7**. Then write your own.

7 7

Trace the word **seven**. Then write your own.

seven

Count and circle the **7** scarecrows. Then try to say the tongue twister **7** times!

Seven sneaky scarecrows

Blue Pool

Color the pool water blue. Then find and circle the 7 objects in this Hidden Pictures® puzzle.

bread   comb   ruler   light bulb   pliers   bowling ball   artist's brush

Kk

This is an uppercase K.

This is a lowercase k.

Trace the uppercase **K**. Then write your own.

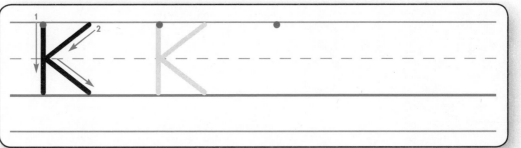

Trace the lowercase **k**. Then write your own.

Now trace **K** and **k** to finish the sentence.

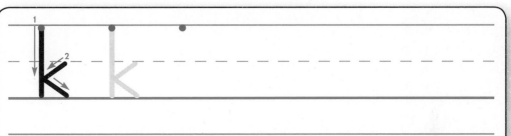

Kate carries

a kayak.

What color is Kate's kayak?

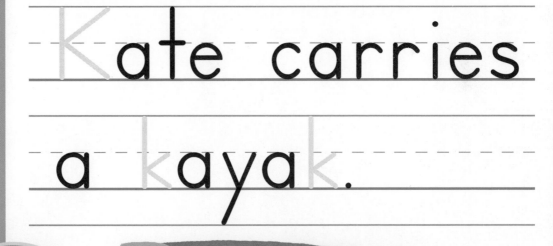

8

eight

This is the number 8.

This is the word **eight**.

This is one way to show 8.

An octopus has **8** arms. Count the arms on each octopus.

Trace the number **8**. Then write your own.

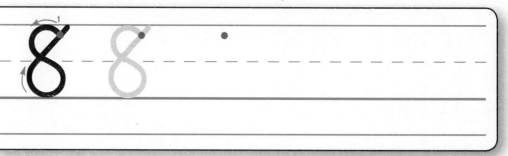

Trace the word **eight**. Then write your own.

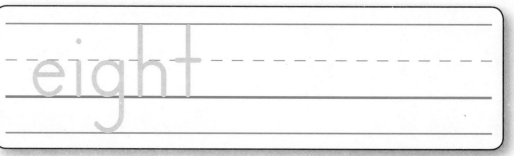

Count the **8** octopuses. Then draw lines between the matching pairs.

Green Frogs

Color the frogs and tree **green**. Then find and circle the **8** objects in this Hidden Pictures® puzzle.

saltshaker

crescent moon

tennis ball

crayon

ladder

spoon

banana

slice of pizza

L l

This is an uppercase **L**.

This is a lowercase **l**.

Trace the uppercase **L**. Then write your own.

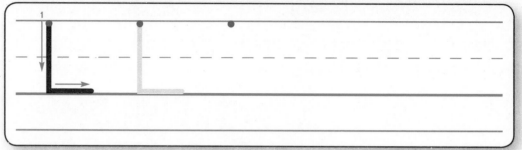

Trace the lowercase **l**. Then write your own.

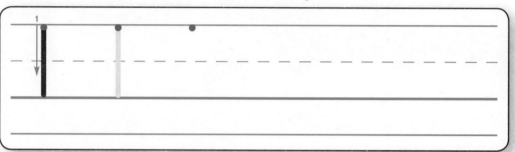

Now trace **L** and **l** to finish the sentence.

Leo likes to sing.

What begins with the letter **L** in this picture?

9
nine

This is the number 9.

This is the word **nine**.

This is one way to show 9.

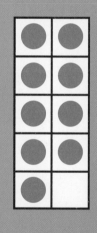

Trace the number **9**. Then write your own.

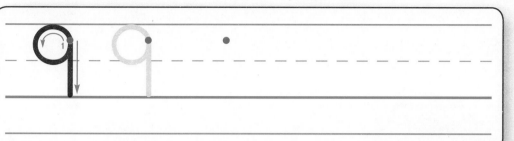

Trace the word **nine**. Then write your own.

nine

Count the **9** ants. Then find and circle the hidden snake, spoon, and crown.

Ovals

An oval is like a stretched circle. Trace the ovals. Color them **green**.

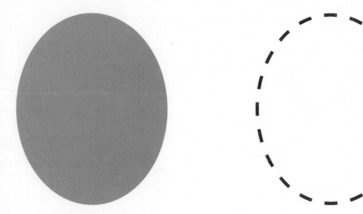

Look at the pictures below.
Draw an oval around each oval you see.

Mm

This is an uppercase M.

This is a lowercase m.

Trace the uppercase **M**. Then write your own.

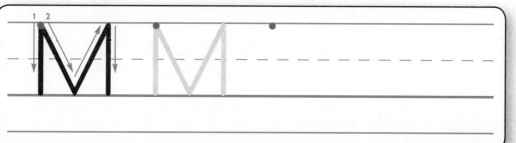

Trace the lowercase **m**. Then write your own.

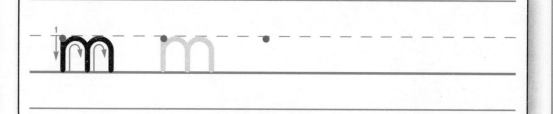

Now trace **M** and **m** to finish the sentence.

Mary hears

music.

What shape are the lenses of Mary's glasses?

Counting: 7 to 9

Find and count: **7** kids, **8** party hats, **9** balloons. Cross off as you go.

Try to say this tongue twister 3 times, fast: *Seth's birthday bash*

Hexagons

A hexagon has 6 sides. Trace the hexagons. Color them **orange**.

Look at the pictures below.
Draw a hexagon around each hexagon you see.

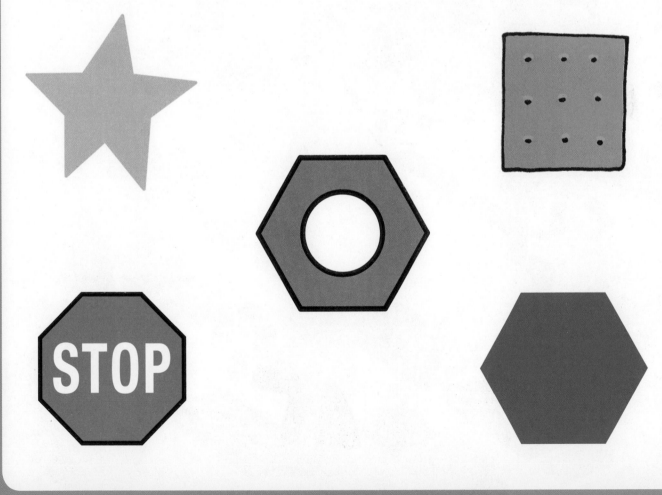

Silly Patterns

The red cans and blue cans make a pattern.
What other patterns do you see?

What silly things do you see?

Nn

This is an uppercase N.

This is a lowercase n.

Trace the uppercase **N**. Then write your own.

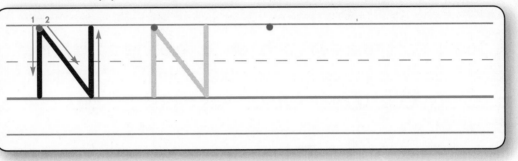

Trace the lowercase **n**. Then write your own.

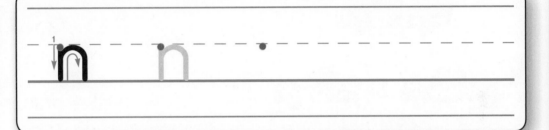

Now trace **N** and **n** to finish the sentence.

Nick needs a napkin.

Compare Sets

Count the 2 groups in each row. Circle the groups that are equal. Need a hint? Draw a line to pair up each object in the first group with one in the second group. If every object has a pair, the groups are equal.

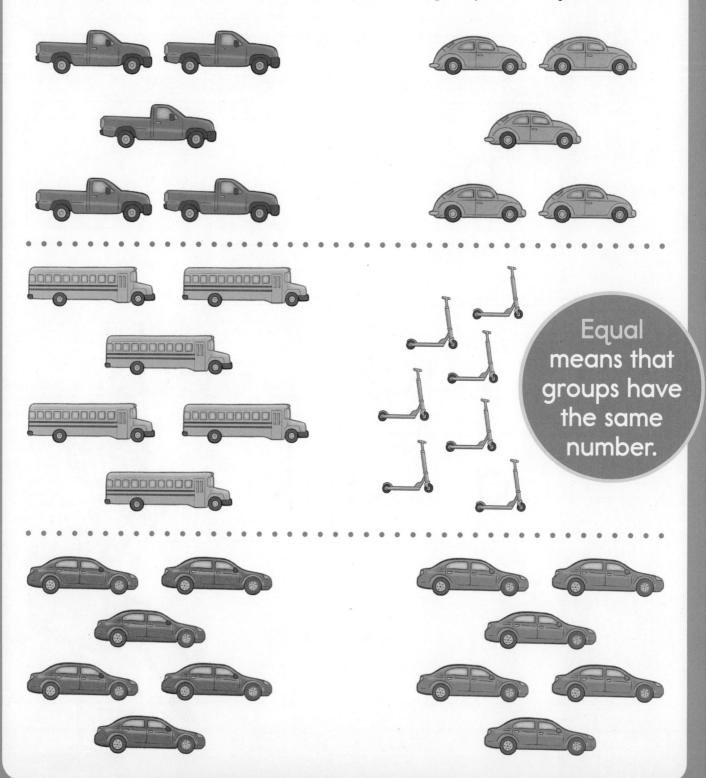

Equal means that groups have the same number.

Picnic Patterns

Circle the object that completes the pattern in each row.

Congratulations! You've completed **Chapter 3**. Place your Chapter 3 sticker on your poster. Try this activity, then start **Chapter 4**!

BONUS!
Summer Craft Activity

Make Your Own Sidewalk-Chalk Stencils

What makes an object easy to trace?

YOU WILL NEED:

- File folders • Pencil • CD case (or other square object)
- Can • Box • Scissors • Sidewalk chalk

1. With an adult's permission, trace a square object on a file folder to make two squares. Draw a line through one to make two triangles.

2. On another file folder, trace around a can to make a circle and around a small box to make a rectangle.

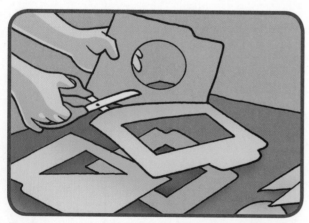

3. Ask an adult to cut out the shapes. Then cut the file folders in half. Now you have four stencils.

4. Use your stencils and sidewalk chalk to make a colorful shape-town.

Oo

This is an uppercase O.

This is a lowercase o.

Trace the uppercase O. Then write your own.

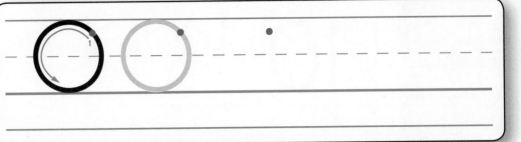

Trace the lowercase o. Then write your own.

Now trace O and o to finish the sentence.

Olivia is an

octopus.

10
ten

This is the number 10.

This is the word **ten**.

This is one way to show 10.

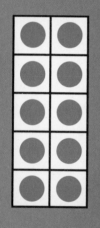

10 10

Trace the word **ten**. Then write your own.

ten

Count the **10** frogs. Then draw a line between each frog and its exact match.

Orange Fish

Color the fish and the flowers **orange**. Then find and circle the **5** objects in this Hidden Pictures® puzzle.

pencil

glove

flag

mushroom

egg

P p

This is an uppercase P.

This is a lowercase p.

Trace the uppercase **P**. Then write your own.

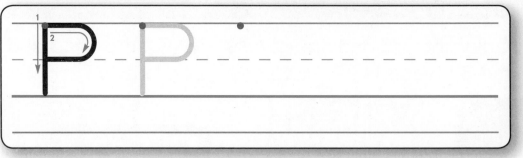

Trace the lowercase **p**. Then write your own.

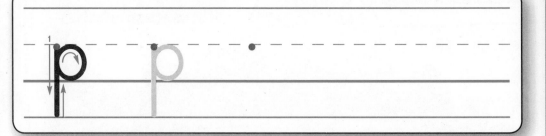

Now trace **P** and **p** to finish the sentence.

Parker and Penny play the piano.

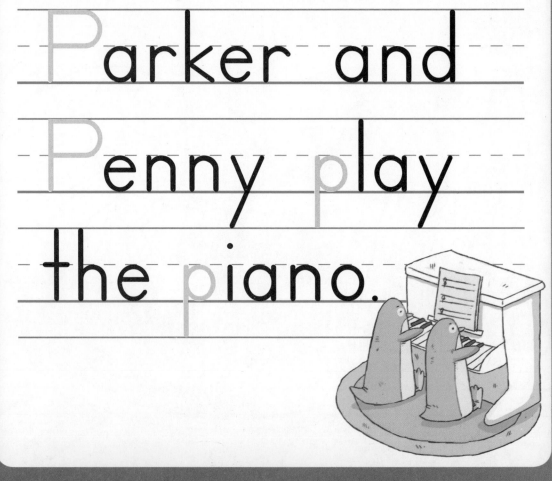

Purple Pig Band

Color the pigs' dresses **purple**. Then find and circle the **6** objects in this Hidden Pictures® puzzle.

Hen and *pen* rhyme. They have the same ending sound. Draw a line between each pair of rhyming objects below.

hen

dish

tie

fish

pen

pie

11
eleven

This is the number 11.

This is the word **eleven**.

This is one way to show 11.

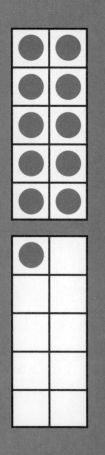

Trace the number 11. Then write your own.

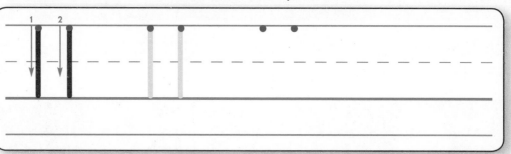

Trace the word **eleven**.

Count the **11** boats. Then find the **11** objects in this Hidden Pictures® puzzle.

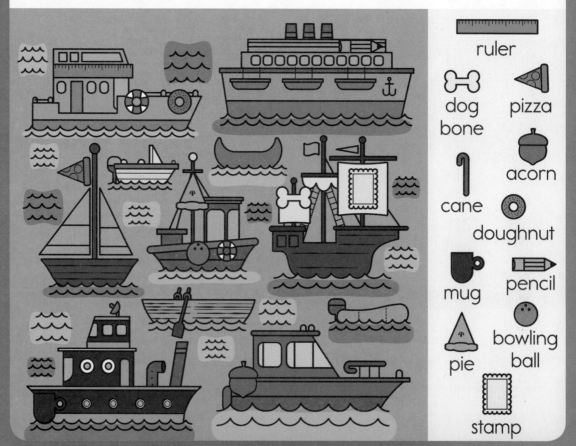

ruler

dog bone

pizza

acorn

cane

doughnut

mug

pencil

pie

bowling ball

stamp

Qq

This is an
uppercase Q.

This is a
lowercase q.

Trace the uppercase **Q**. Then write your own.

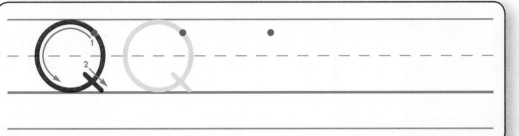

Trace the lowercase **q**. Then write your own.

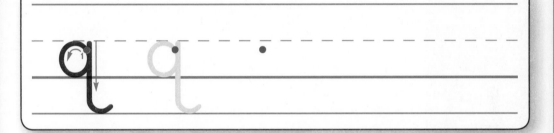

Now trace **Q** and **q** to finish the sentence.

Queen

Quincy

was

quiet.

12
twelve

This is the number 12.

This is the word **twelve**.

This is one way to show 12.

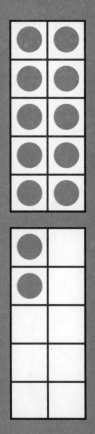

Trace the number **12**. Then write your own.

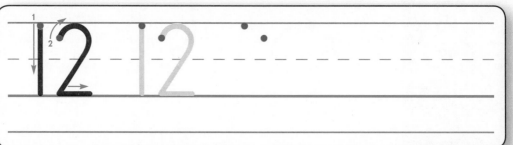

Trace the word **twelve**.

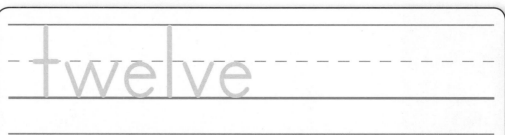

Count **12** pairs of eyeglasses.

What silly things do you see?

Sorting Shapes

Tally marks show how many.					
I	II	III	IIII	IIII̶	IIII̶ I
1	2	3	4	5	6

Count the number of each shape. Make that number of tally marks in the chart below.

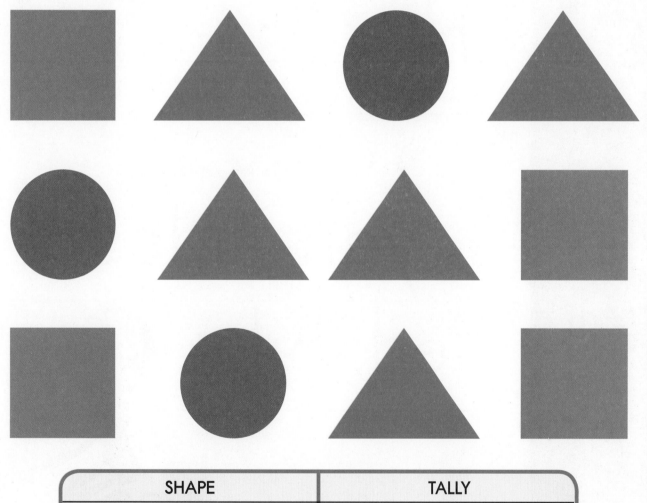

SHAPE	TALLY
▲	
▪	
●	

Rr

This is an uppercase **R**.

This is a lowercase **r**.

Trace the uppercase **R**. Then write your own.

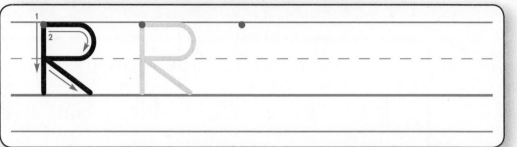

Trace the lowercase **r**. Then write your own.

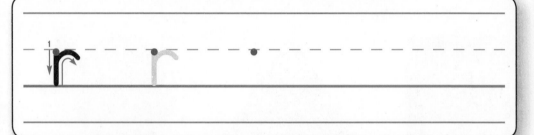

Now trace **R** and **r** to finish the sentence.

Ryan rides a red bike.

Counting: 10 to 12

Find and count: **10** sheep, **11** mugs, **12** pieces of popcorn. Cross off as you go.

Can you find 2 mugs that match exactly?

Classroom Patterns

William's shirt has stripes and Deedee's dress has dots. They are making a pattern with their block tower. What other patterns do you see in the picture?

Look around your home. What patterns do you see inside? What patterns do you see outside?

Color the Shapes

Color all the circles yellow.
Color all the squares green.
Color all the triangles blue.
Color all the rectangles red.

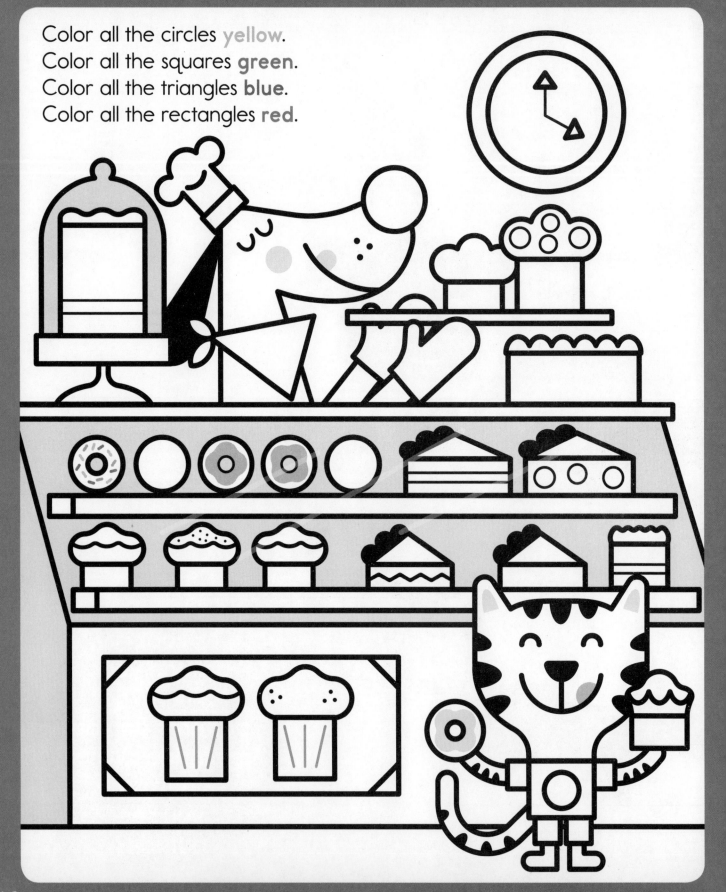

Your Own Pattern

Draw spots on the last ladybug to complete the pattern.

Add spots to these ladybugs to make a pattern.

Draw pepperoni slices on the last pizza to complete the pattern.

Add pepperoni slices to these pizzas to make a pattern.

Monkey Maze

Follow this pattern to help Max get to the big bunch of bananas.

Congratulations! You've completed **Chapter 4**. Place your Chapter 4 sticker on your poster. Try this activity, then start **Chapter 5**!

BONUS!
Summer Fun Recipe

Make a Summer Smoothie!

YOU WILL NEED:
- 20-ounce can crushed pineapple
- 1 cup coconut Greek yogurt
- ½ cup ice chips

1. With an adult's help, pour the pineapple into a strainer. Put ⅔ cup of the drained pineapple into a blender.

2. Add the yogurt and ice chips to the blender. Blend on medium speed until frothy.

3. Pour into a tall glass and enjoy!

Try adding strawberries or a banana to the recipe!

Ss

This is an uppercase S.

This is a lowercase s.

Trace the uppercase **S**. Then write your own.

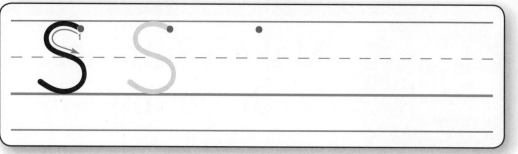

Trace the lowercase **s**. Then write your own.

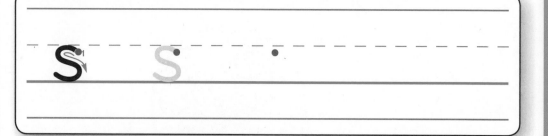

Now trace **S** and **s** to finish the sentence.

Sam swims

in the sea.

13
thirteen

This is the number 13.

This is the word thirteen.

This is one way to show 13.

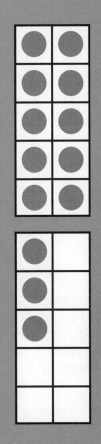

Trace the number 13. Then write your own.

Trace the word **thirteen**.

thirteen

Count the animals in each group, crossing off as you go. Circle the group with 13.

Are there more cats or birds?

Tt

This is an uppercase T.

This is a lowercase t.

Trace the uppercase **T**. Then write your own.

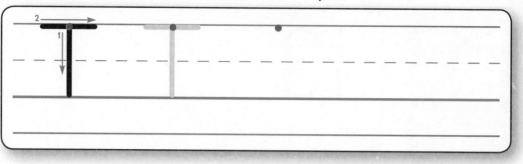

Trace the lowercase **t**. Then write your own.

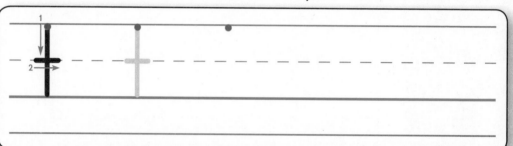

Now trace **T** and **t** to finish the sentence.

Toby paints a turtle.

Do you know what type of bird Toby is?

14

fourteen

This is the number 14.

This is the word fourteen.

This is one way to show 14.

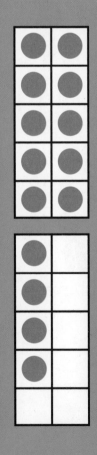

Trace the number 14. Then write your own.

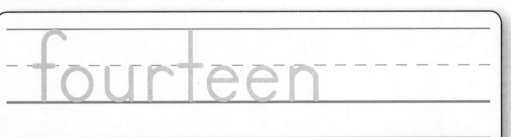

Trace the word **fourteen**.

fourteen

Count the jellybeans in each jar, crossing off as you go. Circle the jar with 14.

Try to say this tongue twister 3 times, fast: *Thomas tried three tangerine jellybeans.*

Brown Dogs

Color each dog **brown**. Then find and circle the **10** objects in this Hidden Pictures® puzzle.

flashlight

pitcher

fish

light bulb

sock

mug

carrot

saltshaker

banana

mitten

15
fifteen

This is the number 15.

This is the word fifteen.

This is one way to show 15.

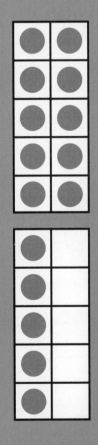

Trace the number 15. Then write your own.

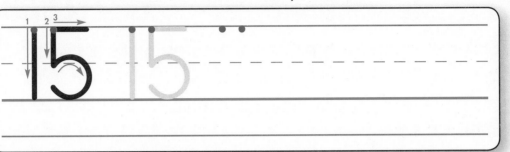

Trace the word **fifteen**.

Count the potatoes. Circle the chef who has 15.

Black and White

Color the pandas **black** on their legs and ears and around their eyes. Be sure to leave the rest of them white. Then find and circle the **8** objects in this Hidden Pictures® puzzle.

slice of bread

snake

flashlight

baseball glove

pencil

corn

car

fish

Uu

This is an uppercase U.

This is a lowercase u.

Trace the uppercase **U**. Then write your own.

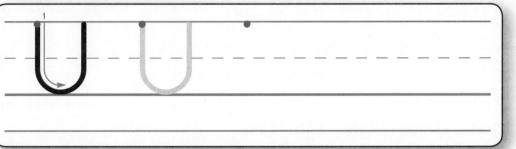

Trace the lowercase **u**. Then write your own.

Now trace **U** and **u** to finish the sentence.

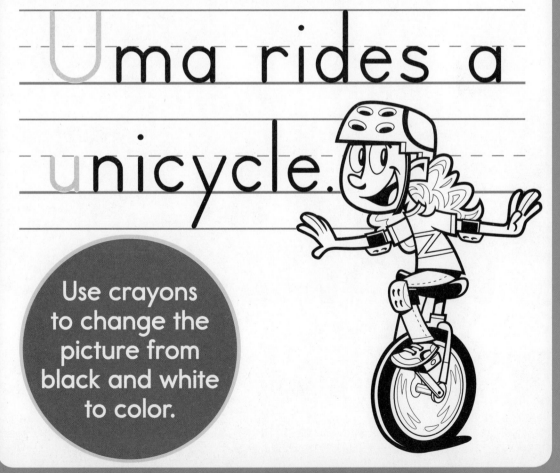

Uma rides a unicycle.

Use crayons to change the picture from black and white to color.

Shape Hunt

What shapes do you see in Grandpa's attic? Look for ◯ circles, ☐ squares, △ triangles, ▭ rectangles, ⬭ ovals, and ⬡ hexagons in this picture.

What else do you see?

Vv

This is an uppercase V.

This is a lowercase v.

Trace the uppercase **V**. Then write your own.

Trace the lowercase **v**. Then write your own.

Now trace **V** and **v** to finish the sentence.

Victor likes to

vacuum.

Counting: 13 to 15

Find and count: **13** people, **14** pieces of cake, **15** cups. Cross off as you go.

3 pairs of people have matching outfits. Can you find them?

Big and Small

Draw a square around the biggest sunflower.
Draw a circle around the smallest zinnia.
Draw a square around the biggest petunia.
Draw a circle around the smallest daisy.

DAISY

PETUNIA

SUNFLOWER

ZINNIA

Tall and Short

Put an X on the tallest bird. Circle the shortest bird.

Long and Short

Put an **X** on the longest worm. Circle the shortest worm.

Rhyme Time

Words that rhyme have the same ending sounds. Say the names of the pictures in each row. Circle the two that rhyme.

cat   hat   dog

clock   cake   snake

log   cow   frog

What Doesn't Belong?

Cross out the thing in each row that doesn't belong. Tell why the other things go together.

We Go Together

Everyone's shoes got mixed up! Draw a line to connect each pair of shoes with the right person.

Congratulations! You've completed **Chapter 5**. Place your Chapter 5 sticker on your poster. Try this activity, then start **Chapter 6**!

BONUS!
Summer Craft Activity

Create Your Own Constellation

Give your constellation its own special name.

YOU WILL NEED:
- Old newspaper or rags
- Rocks
- Paintbrush
- White and black paint
- Glow-in-the-dark paint

1. With an adult's help, cover your work surface with old newspapers or rags. Wash and dry your rocks.

2. Paint white stars on the top of your rocks. Let dry. Paint the stars with glow-in-the-dark paint. Let it dry.

3. Optional: Paint the area around the stars black. Let it dry.

4. Place your rocks in a sunny spot, inside or outside. Arrange the rocks to make your constellation. The stars will soak up the daylight and glow at night.

6

Ww

This is an uppercase W.

This is a lowercase w.

Trace the uppercase **W**. Then write your own.

Trace the lowercase **w**. Then write your own.

Now trace **W** and **w** to finish the sentence.

Wanda has a watch.

16
sixteen

This is the number 16.

This is the word sixteen.

This is one way to show 16.

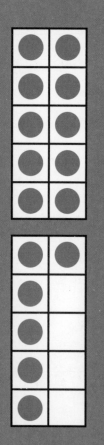

Trace the number 16. Then write your own.

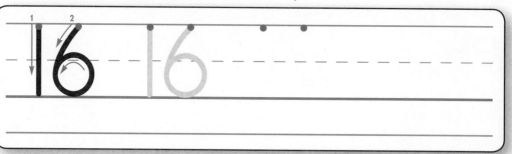

Trace the word **sixteen**.

sixteen

Count the eggs, crossing off as you go. Circle the 2 nests that together have exactly **16** eggs.

Sea Star Sorting

Help sort these sea stars. Draw a line from each one to the pail with the same color.

Which pail will have the most sea stars?

PURPLE

YELLOW

RED

This is an uppercase **X**.

This is a lowercase **x**.

Trace the uppercase **X**. Then write your own.

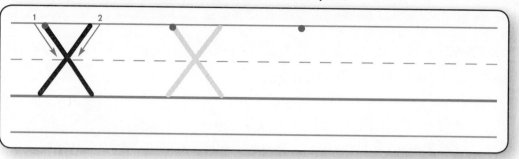

Trace the lowercase **x**. Then write your own.

Now trace **X** and **x** to finish the sentence.

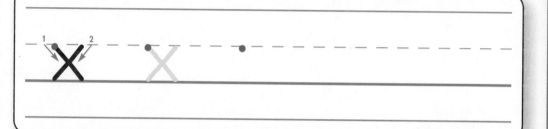

Xavier gets an x-ray.

17
seventeen

This is the number 17.

This is the word **seventeen**.

This is one way to show 17.

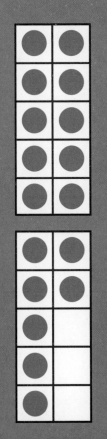

Trace the number **17**. Then write your own.

Trace the word **seventeen**.

seventeen

Count the bees, crossing off as you go. Circle the picture that has exactly **17** bees.

What are 3 words that rhyme with *bee*?

Tall and Short

Draw a circle around the tallest in each group. Put an X on the shortest.

Tell how you know which one is the tallest.

Y y

This is an uppercase Y.

This is a lowercase y.

Trace the uppercase **Y**. Then write your own.

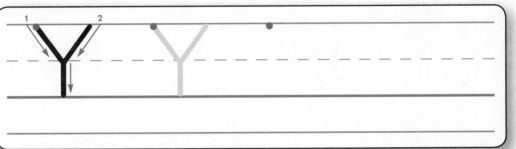

Trace the lowercase **y**. Then write your own.

Now trace **Y** and **y** to finish the sentence.

Yakim has

a yo-yo.

eighteen

This is the number 18.

This is the word **eighteen**.

This is one way to show 18.

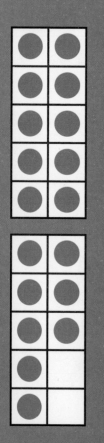

Trace the number **18**. Then write your own.

Trace the word **eighteen**.

eighteen

Count the polka dots. Circle the towel that has **18** polka dots.

Small and Big

Look at each group. Who is the smallest? Who is the biggest? Write **1**, **2**, and **3** to show the order from small to big. We started the first one for you.

Tell how you know which one is the smallest.

Z z

This is an uppercase **Z**.

This is a lowercase **z**.

Trace the uppercase **Z**. Then write your own.

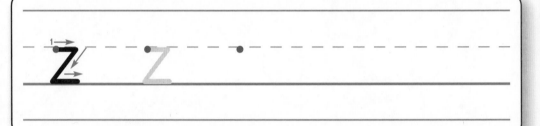

Trace the lowercase **z**. Then write your own.

Now trace **Z** and **z** to finish the sentence.

Zoe lives at the zoo.

Counting: 16 to 18

Count each group of animals, crossing off as you go. Which group has 16? 17? 18?

Which 2 animals start with the same letter?

I Can . . .

I can be big.

I can be small.

I can roll hands fast.

I can roll hands slow.

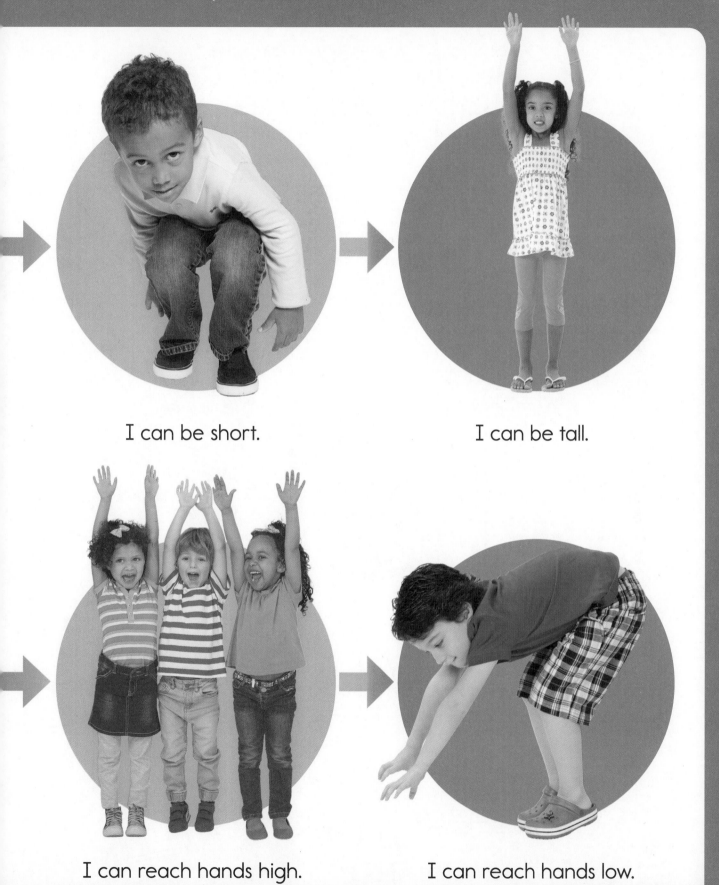

I can be short.

I can be tall.

I can reach hands high.

I can reach hands low.

Lots of Opposites

sailboat

pencil

hat

spoon

domino

fish

Find and circle each of these pairs of opposites in the picture: in and out, big and small, hot and cold, open and closed, high and low, happy and sad.

Now find and color the 12 objects in this Hidden Pictures® puzzle.

artist's brush

pizza

sock

crown

flashlight

scissors

Neighborhood Signs

A traffic light has red, yellow, and green. Draw a line from each color to what it means.

GO

STOP

SLOW

Draw a line from each sign to what it means.

STOP

WALK

BIKE
LANE

BONUS!
Summer Craft Activity

Spread Your Wings

YOU WILL NEED:
- Large piece of cardboard
- Scissors • Foil • Glue
- Paint • Paintbrush • Stickers
- Markers • 2 long pieces of yarn

1. With an adult's help, cut out the shape of butterfly wings from cardboard. Poke four holes in the middle where the wings meet.

2. Cut the foil into small strips. Glue the strips onto the back of the wings and let them dry.

3. Decorate both sides of the wings with paint, stickers, or markers.

4. String each piece of yarn through two holes. Knot the ends of the yarn together.

Look for butterflies around your home. Draw a picture of your favorite.

ABC Food

The kids at Alphabet Academy like foods that start with the same letter as their names. Match each kid with his or her favorite food.

BECKY

EDGAR

CALVIN

PABLO

Name a food that starts with the same letter as your first name.

19
nineteen

This is the number 19.

This is the word nineteen.

This is one way to show 19.

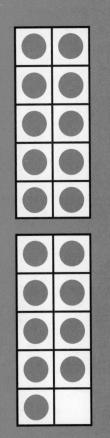

Trace the number 19. Then write your own.

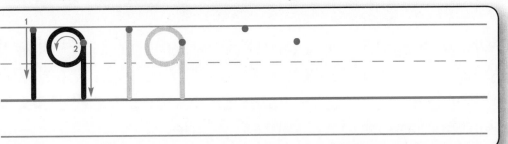

Trace the word **nineteen**.

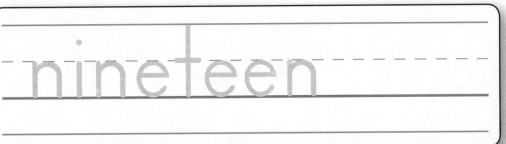

nineteen

Count and color 19 balloons.

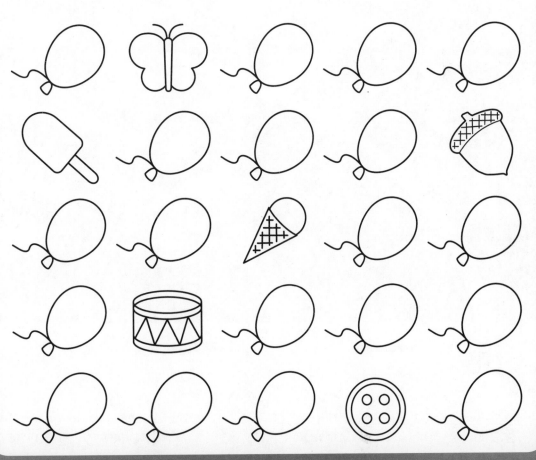

Relay Race

Whose shirt has the letter **D** on it? Where do you see the letter **Q**?
Whose shirt has the letter **X** on it? Where do you see the letter **L**?
Where do you see the letter **Z**? Now find the **9** objects that start
with **R** in this Hidden Pictures® puzzle.

roller
skate   recorder   ribbon   rug   rake

radiator   rattle   raspberry   refrigerator

Super Socks

Which sock has the letter **B** on it? Where do you see the letter **G**? Whose hat has the letter **M** on it? Which sock has the letter **R** on it? How many letter **O**'s can you count in the picture? Now find the **5** objects in this Hidden Pictures® puzzle.

pumpkin

comb

mug

candle

horn

20
twenty

This is the number 20.

This is the word twenty.

This is one way to show 20.

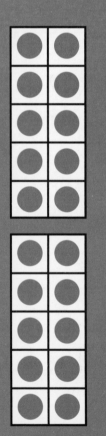

Trace the number **20**. Then write your own.

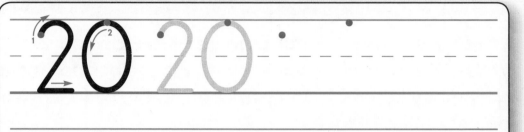

Trace the word **twenty**.

Count the bowling pins, crossing off as you go.
Circle the group that has **20** bowling pins.

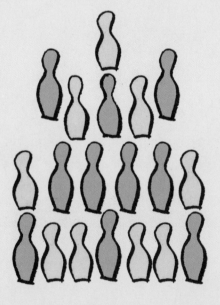

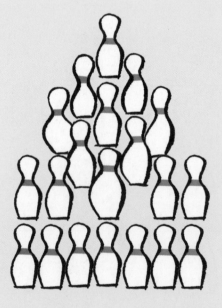

Book Nook

Words that rhyme have the same ending sounds.

Find and circle the **8** objects in this Hidden Pictures® puzzle. Then say the names of the objects. Draw a line between each pair that rhymes.

cupcake

moon

spoon

corn

snowflake

fish

dish

horn

Letter Match-Up

Draw a line to match each uppercase letter to its lowercase letter.

T   B   A   S   H   W   G

h   a   b   g   w   s   t

Alphabet: Uppercase and Lowercase

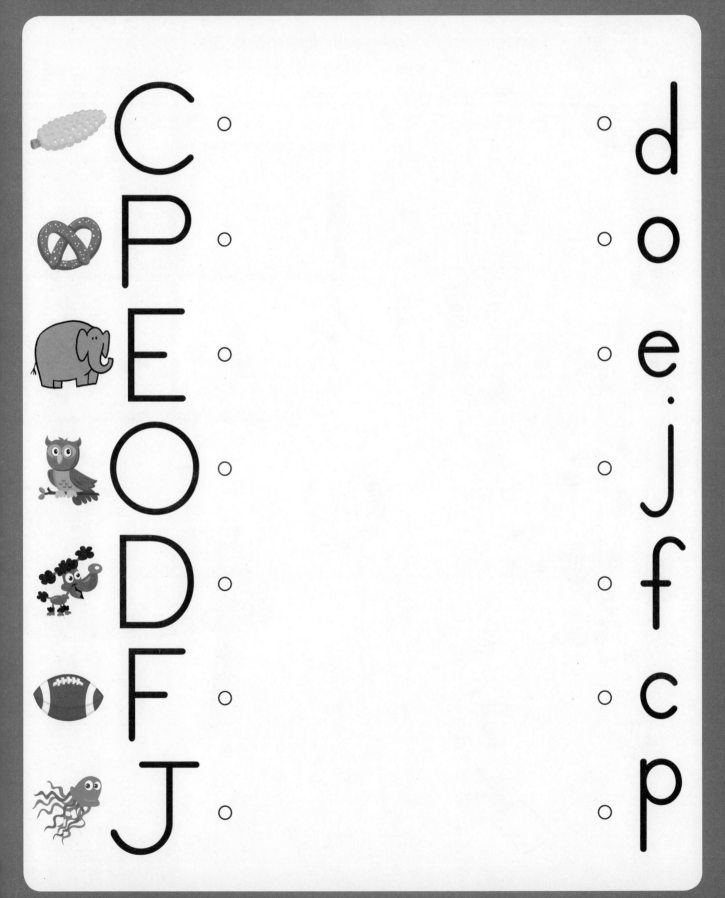

C

P

E

O

D

F

J

d

o

e

j

f

c

p

Which Has the Most?

What silly things do you see?

Circle the cat tower with the most cats.
Circle the cubby with the most dogs.
Circle the fish bowl with the most fish.

Counting: 10 to 20

Count the number of polka dots on each balloon. Color the balloon with **10** polka dots **red**. Color the balloon with **15** polka dots yellow. Color the balloon with **20** polka dots **blue**.

Remember to cross off as you count.

Bird Watching

Color in the boxes to show how many birds of each color there are. Which color has the most?

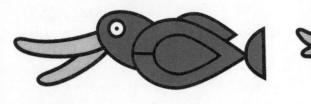

YELLOW						
BLUE						
ORANGE						

Summer Shapes

What shapes do you see in the collage? What shapes would you like to use in a collage?

How many shells can you find?

Which Has Less?

Circle the group in each row that has less frogs.

Math Concepts

See the Signs

It's a busy day at the farmer's market. Draw a line to match each sign to the item for sale.

Carrots Flowers Eggs Jam

How much does the jam cost? How much do the flowers cost?

Lots More!

Without counting, circle the group in each row that has a lot more.

Make Your Own Sets

Gather pennies and paper clips. Then make your own sets that match these.

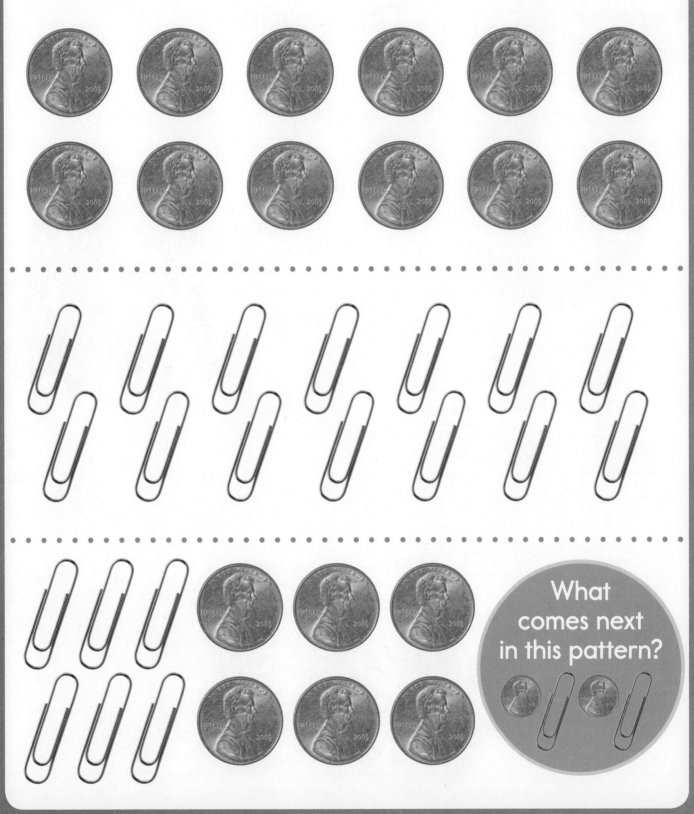

What comes next in this pattern?

BONUS!
Summer Craft Activity

Make Your Own Telescope!

YOU WILL NEED:
- Cardstock
- Cardboard tube
- Rubber bands
- Stickers
- Markers

1. With an adult's help, roll a piece of cardstock over a cardboard tube. Add some rubber bands.

2. Decorate your telescope.

3. Pull the tube to make your telescope longer.

Use your telescope to watch birds. What else can you use it for?

ABC Order

Connect the dots from **A** to **Z** to give this dog a treat.

ABC Order

Sandy is looking for her sandcastle. She can walk only in alphabetical order. Write the missing uppercase letters to help her get there.

abc Order

Zac is heading to meet his friend Zippy. He can travel only in alphabetical order. Write the missing lowercase letters to help Zac reach his friend.

Counting Chickens

Help Farmer Fran count her chickens. Fill in the number of chickens on each hay bale.

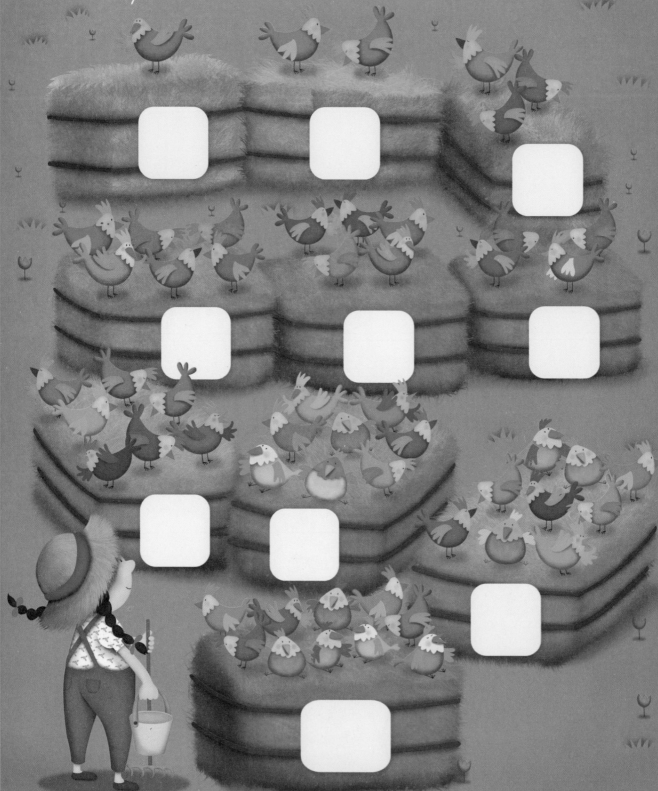

Color Copy

Color the fruit basket to match the one above it.

123 Order

Connect the dots from 1 to 20 to give this girl something fun to slide down.

What is your favorite thing to do at the playground?

abc Order

Connect the dots from **a** to **z** to see a fun way to cook in the summer.

What do you like to eat in the summer?

How Many?

Count the hedgehogs. Then write the number in the box. We did the first one to get you started.

How many hedgehogs?

How many hedgehogs?

How many hedgehogs?

Count the dogs. Then write the number in the box. We did the first one to get you started.

How many dogs?

5

How many dogs?

How many dogs?

Cat at Bat

Find and circle the **8** objects in this Hidden Pictures® puzzle. Say the names of the objects. Draw a line between each pair of rhyming objects.

Words that rhyme have the same ending sounds.

book   rocket   boot   shell   hook   flute   pocket   bell

Fun with Flowers

These pictures are all mixed up. Write the numbers **1**, **2**, and **3** under the pictures to show what happens first, second, and third.

Color these vases. Then draw flowers to fill each vase.

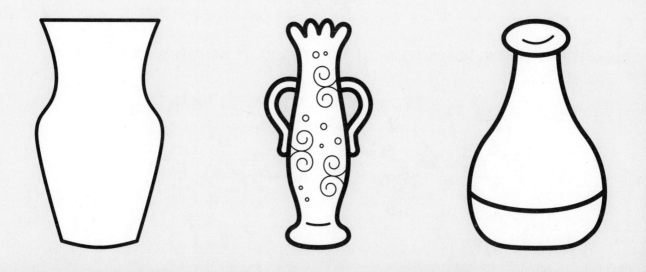

How Many Are Left?

Count the number of flamingos in this row. Cross off **2** flamingos. How many are left? We did this one to get you started.

1

Count the flamingos. Cross off **2** flamingos. How many are left?

Count the flamingos. Cross off **1** flamingo. How many are left?

Count the birds in this row. Cross off **4** birds. How many are left? We did this one to get you started.

0

Count the birds. Cross off **2** birds. How many are left?

Count the birds. Cross off **3** birds. How many are left?

Ship Shape

Find the **12** objects in this Hidden Pictures® puzzle. Name the shape of each object.

tennis ball

candy corn

domino

button

ruler

watermelon

envelope

die

cracker

waffle

slice of pizza

clock

With an empty box and your imagination, you can make lots of fun things. For example, with a parent's permission, a box could turn into:

- a castle
- a clubhouse
- a rocket
- a drum
- a car
- a puppet theater
- a time machine
- a tunnel

What would you make out of a box?

Packing Lunch

These pictures are all mixed up. Write the numbers **1**, **2**, and **3** under the pictures to show what happens first, second, and third.

Draw a line between the **2** lunchboxes that match exactly.

What would you like to pack in your lunchbox?

Congratulations! You've completed **Chapter 8**—and this *Summer Big Fun Workbook.* **GREAT JOB!** Place your Chapter 8 sticker on your poster. Try this activity, then fill out your Achievement Certificate.

BONUS!
Summer
Fun
Recipe

Make Your Own Fruit Pops!

YOU WILL NEED:
- Banana
- Small paper cups
- Craft sticks
- Vanilla yogurt

1. With an adult's permission, peel the banana and cut it into 1-inch slices.

2. Place a banana slice into the bottom of each paper cup and push a craft stick firmly into the fruit.

3. Add yogurt until the cup is almost full.

4. Place the filled cups on a rimmed cookie sheet and put into the freezer for at least 2 hours.

5 Peel off the paper cup and enjoy your "fro-gurt" treat. Use a different fruit next time!

What is your favorite fruit?

Answers

Pages 8–9
Dino Colors

Page 16
Counting: 1 to 3

Page 17
Kite Patterns

Page 19
Shape Patterns

Page 25
Red Apples

Page 28
Yellow Ducks

Page 36
Complete the Pattern

Page 40
Blue Pool

Page 43
Green Frogs

Page 45
9 nine

140

Answers

Page 52
Compare Sets

Page 53
Picnic Patterns

Page 57
Orange Fish

Page 59
Purple Pig Band

hen   dish   tie

pen   fish   pie

Page 60
11 eleven

Page 65
Counting Sheep

Page 76
Brown Dogs

Page 78
Black and White

Page 83
Big and Small

Page 84
Tall and Short

141

Answers

Page 85
Rhyme Time

Page 86
What Doesn't Belong?

Page 87
We Go Together

Pages 102–103
Lots of Opposites

Page 104
Neighborhood Signs

Page 106
ABC Food

Page 108
Relay Race

Page 109
Super Socks

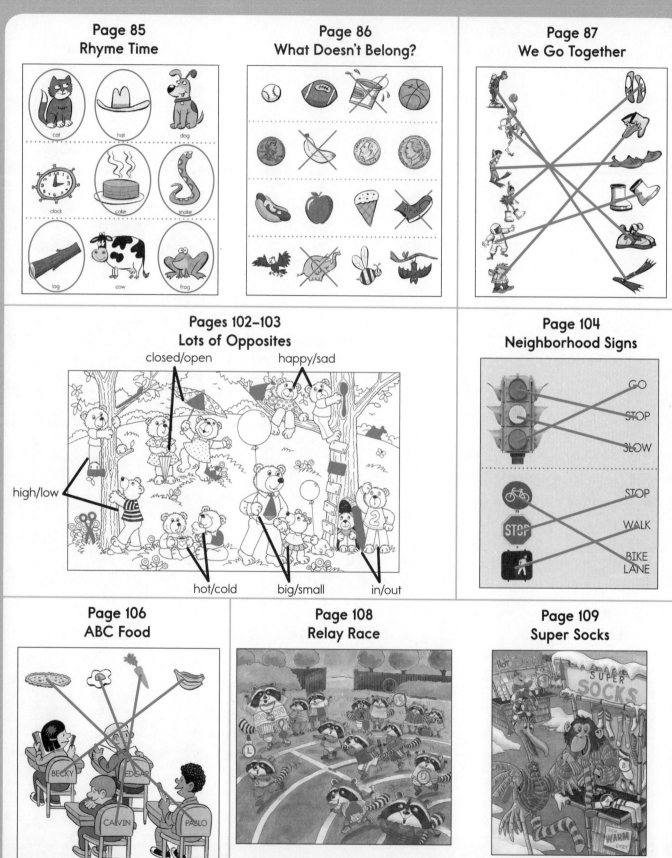

There are 5 O's.

Answers

Page 111
Book Nook

fish cupcake spoon corn
dish snowflake moon horn

Page 114
Which Has the Most?

Page 116
Bird Watching

YELLOW							
BLUE							
ORANGE							

There are 17 birds.

Pages 130–131
How Many?

4 5
5 4
5 6

Page 132
Cat at Bat

book rocket shell flute
hook pocket bell boot

Page 133
Fun with Flowers

2 3 1

Pages 134–135
How Many Are Left?

1 0
2 4
2 2

Pages 136–137
Ship Shape

Page 138
Packing Lunch

2 1 3

Summer Big Fun Adventure Progress Poster

BRIDGING GRADES
P&K

Highlights™

Congratulations!

_____
(your name)

worked hard
and finished the

Summer
Big Fun Workbook

Summer
Big Fun Adventure
Bridging Grades P&K

Start
Place the matching sticker as you finish each chapter.

Chapter 1

GREAT!

C

WEL